Rockets Galore!

Rockets
Old and New

Rockets were first invented by the ancient Chinese. They combined sulfur, saltpeter, and charcoal to create explosive gunpowder.

Although today's rockets are huge compared with those early Chinese ones, they work in much the same way – a controlled explosion at the back of the rocket blasts it into the air.

Arrow Launcher
By about AD 1000 the Chinese were using the explosive power of gunpowder to make hand-held multiple arrow launchers. These were very powerful weapons in their day.

Launch Platform
When the British were at war with the French emperor Napoleon Bonaparte, about 200 years ago, they used mobile launch platforms like this to fire rockets at the enemy soldiers.

Saturn V

In use between 1967 and 1972, NASA's Saturn V rocket was commonly known as the Moon Rocket. Here seen "exploded" into its component parts, the rocket stood 364 feet tall.

V2 Rocket

The V2 rocket was developed by the Germans during the final years of World War II. It looks very much like a modern rocket and it stood 45 feet tall.

Space Shuttle

Standing 185 feet tall, the NASA Space Shuttle is unique because it is the world's first reusable space vehicle, although its enormous external fuel tank, which powers it into orbit, is discarded.

United States X33

Rocket Plane

Still at the planning stage, this NASA craft might one day take its passengers out of the Earth's atmosphere into near space, wait as the world spins beneath it, and then come down again when ready to land.

Amazing Facts

A woodpecker once delayed the launch of the Space Shuttle simply by doing what a woodpecker does – it pecked more than 75 separate holes in the casing around the fuel tank!

Rocket Power

When a rocket roars off into the atmosphere, it is powered by a blast of hot gases from its tail pushing against the air.

In space, though, where there is no air, how does the rocket fly? It does this because of what is known as "action and reaction" – as a reaction to the hot gases rushing backward out of the engines, the rocket is pushed forward in the opposite direction.

An Ariane rockets (seen in cutaway form) lifts off from its launch pad. The flags of the participating countries in the European Space Agency are on its side.

Did you know?

The three-stage Saturn V rocket weighs 6,699,000 pounds and it produces 7,648,000 pounds of take-off thrust.

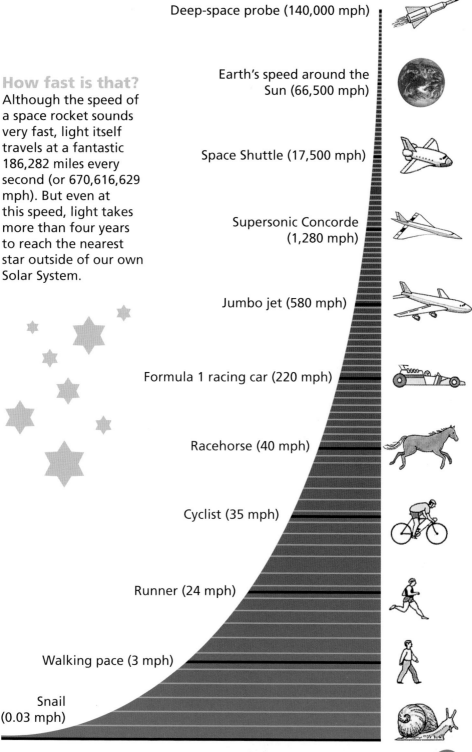

Deep-space probe (140,000 mph)

Earth's speed around the Sun (66,500 mph)

Space Shuttle (17,500 mph)

Supersonic Concorde (1,280 mph)

Jumbo jet (580 mph)

Formula 1 racing car (220 mph)

Racehorse (40 mph)

Cyclist (35 mph)

Runner (24 mph)

Walking pace (3 mph)

Snail (0.03 mph)

How fast is that?

Although the speed of a space rocket sounds very fast, light itself travels at a fantastic 186,282 miles every second (or 670,616,629 mph). But even at this speed, light takes more than four years to reach the nearest star outside of our own Solar System.

Make a Water Rocket

The water in this project is used to provide the mass needed to give your water rocket a mighty thrust. This should lift the body of the rocket high into the air.

You will need

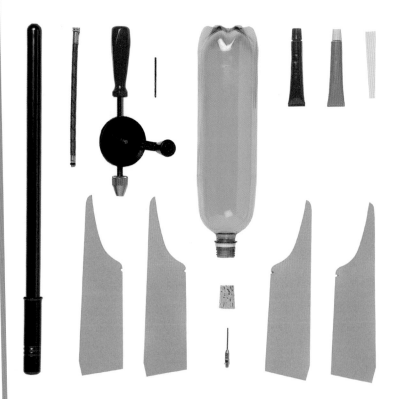

- Bicycle pump and connector
- Needle adaptor (used for pumping up basketballs, footballs, etc)
- Drill and bit
- Large plastic soda bottle
- Epoxy glue
- Balsa wood cut into 4 fin shapes
- Cork, shaped to fit bottle

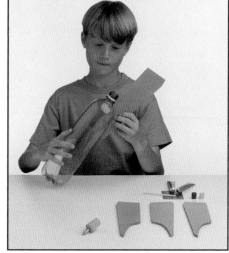

1 Under adult supervision, carefully drill a hole in the cork wide enough for the needle adaptor to make a good, tight fit. Push in the needle from the wide end, keeping your fingers out of danger.

2 Cut the fin shapes out of the balsa wood. Glue them to the rocket and allow them to dry. The fins support the rocket while you pump in the air and help it to fly straight.

3 Quarter fill the bottle with water, push the cork firmly in, and connect the pump. Take your rocket out into the open, away from buildings and overhead wires. Stand your rocket up on its fins on a good, even surface. Standing back as far as you can, pump air into the rocket. As the pressure builds up the cork will pop out and then ... BLAST OFF!

Games and Puzzles

Space Quiz

Looking at the stories in this Activity booklet, can you answer the following questions?

1 Which civilization first invented the rocket?..

2 Which travels faster:

☐ **A** a supersonic Concorde   ☐ **B** the Space Shuttle?

3 How fast does a rocket have to be moving to get into orbit?

....

4 How fast does a rocket have to be moving to
break free of the Earth's gravity and travel into space?.........................

5 Why was the Space Shuttle such an important development?

....

Answers:
Page 16

Did you know?

In space, due to the lack of
gravity, astronauts grow a little
and they are up to three-
quarters of an inch taller
than they are on Earth.

Word Search
Find all these words hidden in the square

Astronaut
Rocket
Atmosphere
Shuttle
Pilot
Friction
Fuel
NASA
Launch
Orbit
Speed
Fire
Probe

P	X	D	F	P	A	T	F	R	I	C	T	I	O	N
N	I	A	C	B	S	Z	K	Q	P	N	F	G	I	E
C	J	L	L	F	T	M	S	P	E	E	D	D	R	L
F	S	T	O	U	R	B	V	Y	E	J	L	E	K	T
G	T	P	N	T	O	V	C	W	S	F	H	M	J	R
K	A	I	H	P	N	P	T	A	J	P	D	S	O	A
O	B	P	L	J	A	J	W	B	S	T	F	A	L	C
A	R	Q	O	K	U	D	R	O	I	P	G	Q	G	T
Z	L	B	W	F	T	Q	M	K	R	O	C	K	E	T
L	P	D	I	S	I	T	F	P	P	M	J	P	D	U
A	A	K	G	T	A	U	H	C	F	I	R	E	S	M
U	C	P	R	O	B	E	B	X	B	N	L	L	F	X
N	S	M	T	V	N	A	S	A	S	F	C	J	U	A
C	I	Z	W	O	L	L	C	E	T	G	V	S	E	E
H	L	S	H	U	T	T	L	E	L	H	Z	W	L	R

Controlled Flight

Attach short straws firmly to one side of an inflated balloon. Run a piece of fine thread through the straws and fix it at an angle between two points. Make sure the thread is good and tight. Then release the air from the balloon and watch it fly right up the thread!

Aboard the Shuttle

It wasn't that long ago that stories about space flight were just science fiction. Now, spacecraft such as the Space Shuttle regularly blast off from Earth.

The Space Shuttle performs many different jobs. Much of its work consists of launching satellites, such as weather or telecommunications satellites, into orbit. Astronauts also leave the Shuttle to do jobs outside in space itself. One of these has been to make repairs to the Hubble Space Telescope. Launched in 1990, and weighing more than 24,000 pounds, the telescope needs regular maintenance to keep it working.

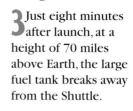

3 Just eight minutes after launch, at a height of 70 miles above Earth, the large fuel tank breaks away from the Shuttle.

2 The booster rockets fall away at about 29 miles high. They are recovered from the sea and used again.

1 To lift the Shuttle into space, its own rocket engines fire, as well as booster engines on the side. To get into orbit, a spacecraft must reach a speed of 17,500 mph.

Did you know?

In order to break free from Earth's gravitational pull and travel into space, a spacecraft must reach a speed of 25,000 mph – that is nearly 7 miles per second!

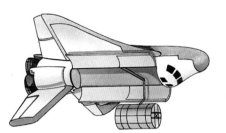

4 Once in orbit, the Shuttle can start work on the tasks assigned to that mission. One common job is launching satellites, using its robot arm.

5 At the end of its mission, the Shuttle turns around and fires its engines to slow down and begin its descent back to Earth.

7 When the Shuttle is in the atmosphere, the pilot flies the ship home. But it has no power now. It is, in fact, an enormous glider!

6 When the Shuttle enters the atmosphere, friction with the air makes the heat-resistant underside of the ship glow red hot.

International Space Station

One of the most important jobs for the Space Shuttle for the last few years has been taking equipment, supplies, and crew into orbit to help build and maintain the International Space Station. The Space Station is a joint project with the USA, Russia, Japan, Canada, and some countries in Europe.

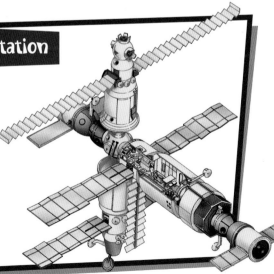

Alien Blast-off

The police cruiser raced along the highway at Socorro, New Mexico. It was 5.45 pm and Officer Lonnie Zamora was in pursuit of a Chevrolet traveling way above the local speed limit, clouds of dust being thrown up from the vehicle's speeding tires.

Suddenly Lonnie caught sight of an extraordinary blue-orange flame in the sky, which then flew down behind a nearby hill. Turning his cruiser away from the road, he sped off across country to where the flame had disappeared.

As Lonnie drew nearer, he noticed an odd-looking object. At first he thought it was an upside-down car. Climbing out of his own car to take a closer look, the object seemed to be an egg-shaped ship, with no windows or doors, resting on four silver legs. Near the craft, Lonnie saw two child-sized figures dressed from head to toe in white coveralls. One of the figures then saw Lonnie and jumped, as if in surprise. Who – or what – could they be?

Getting back in his car, Lonnie radioed the sheriff's office for help, but when he looked up again the two little figures had disappeared. Hearing loud thumps from inside the craft, Lonnie approached closer, and then a loud blast filled the desert air.

The craft began to rise from the ground, sending up a whirlwind of dust. The engine noise changed, but it was nothing like that of a plane. Lonnie, thinking the ship was about to explode, dived for cover. But instead of blowing up, it shot up into the sky like a bullet and vanished.

Police Sergeant Sam Chavez reached Officer Lonnie Zamora just after the craft blasted off, and some nearby bushes were still burning. Making a thorough search of the area, the two policemen found scorch marks on the ground together with four round dents in the soil where the craft's legs had rested. They also found five other marks that looked like footprints.

Two days later, another witness saw a craft land at La Madera, New Mexico. Local police officers found evidence of burning where the witness reported the craft had come down. They also found four round prints in the soil, just as they had at Socorro.

These two sightings were made in 1964 and they are just two of the hundreds of reports that are made each year by people who claim to have seen Unidentified Flying Objects (UFOs) or alien beings. Sightings have been made in North and South America, parts of Asia, Africa, Australia, Europe, and Scandinavia. What do you think?

Sky Rockets

Independence Day on July 4 and New Year's Eve on December 31 are probably the days when you see the biggest fireworks displays in the United States.

In other countries, however, important national days are also celebrated with fireworks and skyrockets. The first skyrockets were invented by the Chinese, and the next Chinese New Year will be on February 7, 2008.

Guy Fawkes Night

On November 5 every year throughout Britain, firework displays commemorate the failed Gunpowder Plot when, in 1605, conspirators, including Guy Fawkes, attempted to blow up Parliament in Westminster, central London, and kill the king.

Be Safe

All fireworks and skyrockets are designed to explode and are potentially dangerous. Never play with matches or light a firework without adult supervision.

Up, Up and Away

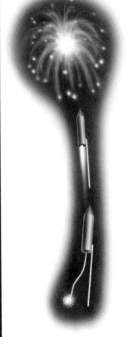

Stable flight

The stick used to support the skyrocket before lift-off also helps it to fly straight and true up into the air before exploding.

Answers
Space Quiz: **1** Chinese; **2** Space Shuttle; **3** 17,500 mph; **4** 25,000 mph; **5** Because it is reusable